THE CHURCH OF THE HOLY GHOST

Ludmilla Bollow

BROADWAY PLAY PUBLISHING INC
New York
www.broadwayplaypublishing.com
info@broadwayplaypublishing.com

THE CHURCH OF THE HOLY GHOST
© Copyright 1995 by Ludmilla Bollow

All rights reserved. This work is fully protected under the copyright laws of the United States of America. No part of this publication may be photocopied, reproduced, stored in a retrieval system, or transmitted, in any form or by any means, electronic, mechanical, recording, or otherwise, without the prior permission of the publisher. Additional copies of this play are available from the publisher.

Written permission is required for live performance of any sort. This includes readings, cuttings, scenes, and excerpts. For amateur and stock performances, please contact Broadway Play Publishing Inc. For all other rights please contact the author at 314 W Sugar Lane, Milwaukee, WI 53217.

Cover photo by Jeri Schwartz

I S B N: 978-0-88145-119-1
First printing: December 1995
This printing: December 2016

Book design: Marie Donovan
Page make-up: Adobe Indesign
Typeface: Palatino

CHARACTERS

ERIN, *mother, early thirties*
HEATHER, *daughter, around ten*
SANDRA, *neighbor, nearing forty*
JERICO, *former preacher, middle-aged*
MAN, *wears a hooded dark-gray sweatjacket that shadows his facial features, so age or appearance is not discernible.*

Time: *Early fall*

Place: *Converted church on the edge of a small Midwestern town*

ACT ONE:
Scene One: *Late evening*
Scene Two: *A few days later*
Scene Three: *Later that evening*
Scene Four: *Following night*

ACT TWO:
Scene One: *One week later*
Scene Two: *A few hours later*
Scene Three: *One month later*
Scene Four: *A few minutes later*

To: Patty and Roger Gross
For their dedication to Playwrights and the Theater
And fostering the Mount Sequoyah New Play Retreat

ACT ONE

Scene One

(Interior of a one-room wooden church converted into living quarters.)

(At first glance it might not be recognized as a church, except for a single stained-glass gothic window that rises above the tops of the bookshelves lining the back wall. Left section of shelves is overflowing with stuffed animals. Right shelves house a collection of vases in unusual shapes, sizes, and colors. Atop are vases filled with dried flowes, field grasses, and bright crepe paper blossoms. The other windows have been boarded over, either to conserve heat or because they were too expensive to replace.)

(Left corner, an old pot-bellied stove, firewood nearby. Oblong table with chairs, computer and accessories set up on one end. Small T V, recliner, and inexpensive furniture complete the rest of the sparsely furnished, yet comfortable-looking room.)

(Stage right is door to the outside, stage left door to an old dirt basement where furnace is housed. On back wall, to right of bookshelves is bathroom door. Left of shelves is open doorway area to kitchen, storeroom, and stairway to the choirloft, which has been converted into two sleeping areas. Stairs continue up into open church belfry.)

(Before curtain rise: Organ music plays distantly. Country church voices rise faintly, singing chorus of Come to the Church in the Wildwood.*)*

CHORUS: Oh come, come, come, come—
Come to the church in the Wildwood,
Oh come to the church in the dale,
No spot is so dear to my childhood,
As the little brown church in the vale…

*(*CHORUS *continues with "Come, come, come…" in monotone repeats.)*

(Voices blend into amplified computer clicks and beeps which are the only sounds heard as curtain rises.)

(At rise, ERIN, *dressed casually, shoes off, seated at computer, in deep concentration, workbook open before her. She pauses, looks about as if hearing something, then continues.)*

HEATHER: *(Offstage)* Mom—Mom—

*(*HEATHER *appears in stairway door. She is about ten, wearing a long flannel nightgown, dragging a large stuffed green frog with bubble eyes and floppy webbed feet.)*

HEATHER: Mom—when you coming up to bed?

ERIN: *(Not pausing)* When I'm through. One more lesson. Okay? And if you don't keep bothering me I'll get done that much faster.

HEATHER: Can I stay down here and wait for you?

ERIN: No—I need to concentrate—alone.

HEATHER: I won't talk to you.

ERIN: You are, now.

HEATHER: I can't sleep.

ERIN: And I can't work.

HEATHER: *(Pause)* I heard the music again.

ACT ONE

ERIN: All right, stay down here. But no talking. Not a peep!

(HEATHER *silently goes to bookshelves and begins playing with stuffed animals. Goes into soft mimicking voices of various tones as if animals were talking to one another in a strange language.*)

ERIN: *(Admonishing)* Heather—

HEATHER: It's not me talking, it's my animals—Pink Panther and Beetlejuice. They don't like it down here, all alone at night—with that big eye watching over them. *(Points to window)* They want to go to bed with me.

ERIN: There isn't room for one more animal in that bed of yours.

HEATHER: Under my bed. They want to go under my bed—and fill up all those dark spaces—so there's no room under there for any more monsters, and—

ERIN: Heather, please—

(HEATHER *stops, then whispers softly as if the animals were talking to one another in same strange language.*)

ERIN: All right. All right. I'll get up early and finish. This damn computer is doing all kinds of crazy things anyway.

HEATHER: *(Comes over quickly with Polly Wolly)* Can I try, Mom?

ERIN: I'm only renting it—I don't want it broken.

HEATHER: But I know how. We use them at the new school. Let me show you.

ERIN: Okay. One sentence, then off you go. No ifs, ands, or buts.

HEATHER: Polly Wolly wants to try, okay? *(Sits importantly at table. Positions frog so his hands hit the keys.)*

ERIN: Why not. Maybe he can work it better than me.

HEATHER: *(Singing in deep frog voice as frog hits various keys)* I'm working at the computer— "Ribbit—Ribbit" He can't spell "Ribbit". He's having trouble—

(All of a sudden wild computer sounds are heard and flashes and pictures jump on the screen)

ERIN: *(Turns machine off.)* I told you this computer is not a toy! It breaks, I have to pay for it! That's it—to bed. Immediately!

HEATHER: *(Begins sobbing)* Now you're mad at me.

ERIN: Yes, I am.

HEATHER: And I won't be able to sleep. I can never sleep in this place. I don't know why we moved here.

ERIN: We're not going into that again.

HEATHER: I wanted to stay at Grandma's. Why did we have to move away from Cricket Bay anyways. My animals liked it there, and—

ERIN: Because Grandma died—the house was sold—

HEATHER: I had my own room there. And I wasn't afraid.

ERIN: There's nothing to be afraid of here.

HEATHER: Yes, there is.

ERIN: Whatever it is—I can't do anything about it.

HEATHER: You could be nicer to me.

ERIN: I try. That's all I can do, is try… Want me to sing to you?

HEATHER: Yeah. Grandma always sang to me. Every night.

ACT ONE 5

ERIN: Come on. *(Takes* HEATHER *to sofa. Holds her, rocks her.)*
Oh, I went down South for to see my gal,
Singing Polly Wolly Doodle all the day—
Oh my Heather am a purty little gal…

*(*HEATHER *joins in.)*

ERIN & HEATHER:
Singing Polly Wolly Doodle all the day.
Fare thee well. Fare thee well,
Fare thee well to Cricket Bay—
Oh we're going to Indiana, maybe live in Texarkana,
Singing Polly Wolly Doodle all the day…

HEATHER: You sing better than Grandma.

ERIN: Thanks. *(Gets up)* Let me check things, then we'll both go up together. *(Checks door locks, lights, etc.)*

HEATHER: I still hear the organ at night—honest.

ERIN: I explained—it's from the new church—the one up on the hill. Wind carries the sound, and—

HEATHER: It's from this church. Somewhere inside of this church.

ERIN: This is a house, not a church. Our house. I bought it—I'm paying for it, and as soon as I can afford it, you won't know in any way that it ever was a church.

HEATHER: I'll know. The kids at school know.

ERIN: That's it. Enough already! We are staying here. We are not moving! All those tricks of your imagination are not going to make me feel guilty; make me move; keep me from earning a living. Your bedtime is nine-thirty, do you hear me. Every night you are going to be in bed at nine-thirty. We've been living here three months already, so you should be used to sleeping in your room by now. *(Goes back to computer. Turns it on.)*

HEATHER: It's not a room—it's a choir loft. And people still sing up there.

ERIN: Well, don't listen! Shut down that imagination of yours at least when you go to bed.

HEATHER: You don't believe me anymore! Grandma always believed me.

ERIN: You are not Grandma's baby anymore! It's just you and me from hereon in. Nobody else to help us—nobody. *(Puts hands over eyes)*

HEATHER: Don't cry Mom—

ERIN: I don't know all the answers—so how can I tell you answers.

HEATHER: It's okay, Mom—I'll go to bed.

ERIN: I'm sorry, Heather. *(Holds her)*

HEATHER: It's okay. Just don't cry anymore. Polly Wolly doesn't want you to cry either.

ERIN: Okay, I won't. At least I'll try harder not to. We both have to try harder, don't we.

HEATHER: Yeah we do. *(Hugs* ERIN. *Exits.)* `Night mom. We'll leave the lights on for you.

ERIN: I'll be up in a minute.

*(*ERIN *goes to computer. Rests head in hands. Accidentally hits computer keys. Noises and flashes go off. Alerted, she turns machine off. Closes book. Pauses. Organ music is heard very faintly. Looks around.)*

ERIN: It has to be coming from that other church. There is no other explanation.

(Music rises louder. Presses fingers in her ears.)

ERIN: Noo—noo—I have to keep my sanity. I can't lose that again. I can't...

(End Scene One)

ACT ONE

Scene Two

(*A few days later.* SANDRA *is standing inside doorway, still huffing from running. She is older than* ERIN, *dressed in colorful jogging suit.*)

SANDRA: I run past here every day and every day I've been meaning to stop—I'm Sandra Porter, live down the road—the peach house.

ERIN: Hi. I'm Erin—Erin McCann.

SANDRA: I said to myself, geez, you should take some pie or cake over to welcome your new neighbor. But—I work—and I run—and I try to run my house too—while my husband travels all over, and does who knows what. I don't even bake for my own family. (*Plops in recliner, making herself at home*)

ERIN: I'm just in the midst of fixing supper—meatloaf. Would you like a cup of coffee?

SANDRA: Tea. Herbal tea's all I drink now. (*Makes face*) Anyway, I run by this church all the time and—

ERIN: It's a house. Our house.

SANDRA: I know, but I been raised in this town, and to me it's always gonna be a church. God—what was its name— "Church of the Holy—" something.

ERIN: Doesn't matter—all in the past.

SANDRA: (*Takes shoes off, rubs feet*) Anyways, I wondered who was living here now. Then my little girl, Jennifer, she says there's a new girl in her class at Jefferson School, who lives in the church—

ERIN: House.

SANDRA: House—and I thought, well geez, I should go and say "Hi" or something. You know, I would appreciate a glass of water. That I'm allowed.

(ERIN *exits.* SANDRA *snoops with her eyes.* ERIN *returns with water.*)

ERIN: Need ice?

SANDRA: Nah. This is fine. You drink the well water here?

ERIN: Yes. It's been tested.

SANDRA: Tastes okay—I guess. You don't need to know all what went on here before. About the last "family".

ERIN: No, I don't think I do.

SANDRA: You got other kids?

ERIN: Just Heather.

SANDRA: Noticed all those stuffed critters. Enough there for twenty kids.

ERIN: Heather's family.

SANDRA: And she sleeps with them—

ERIN: As many as she can.

SANDRA: I don't let Jennifer sleep with hers anymore. They gotta grow up—sometime. Not quick enough for me.

ERIN: Well, Heather—her life— *(Stops)* They're her security blanket. I would never take away anyone's security blanket—not till they're ready.

SANDRA: Oh. *(Pause)* And you must collect vases.

ERIN: I used to. Made them too—and flowers.

SANDRA: Lots of rummage sales 'round this burg. You can pick up all the old "vahses" you want.

ERIN: I think I have enough, don't you.

SANDRA: Yep. Sure made this place cozy. Shoulda seen it before.

ERIN: Price was right.

ACT ONE

SANDRA: I bet… Your husband come home for supper?

ERIN: I don't have a husband.

SANDRA: Oh. Divorced?

ERIN: No. I don't have a husband.

SANDRA: Hey, I'm not gonna pry. May have heard about nosey small town people. But I'll tell you the truth, I'm much too busy for coffee klatsching. Hell, I got four kids to raise—and every day, 'bout this time, I need to get out and run, or bust my guts. My ma—she used to yak on the phone to escape us kids. Me—I run—and scream all my problems to the wind.

ERIN: Look, why don't you stop by another time. I have class this evening, and I have to finish supper.

SANDRA: Class?

ERIN: At Deerwood School. Computer classes—so I can advance in my job.

SANDRA: I heard you work at the courthouse. *(Walks around, obviously inspecting)*

ERIN: That's what brought me here. Took a state civil service test. Got a really high score—and the first opening was here in Jefferson City. So, I had to find a place real quick, one I could afford. Now, if I can just pass these computer tests—I move up one more job grade, and get more money.

SANDRA: Go for it! *(Looking at computer)* These things scare the hell out of me. Wash machines, with all their lights and cycles, 'bout all I can handle. Then, the old man, he gives me a microwave for my birthday. Wasn't for me—for him—so he'd get his damn meals quicker, no matter what time he dragged home. I tell you—

ERIN: I really have to—

SANDRA: I know, you're busy, so am I. But, well, there is one thing I did want to talk to you about, and since you don't have a phone—

ERIN: Next month. They promise me one by then.

SANDRA: Anyways, I just thought you should know, and you can take care of it in your own way—but, well, I'm only repeating kids' talk—Heather around?

ERIN: She went to the store.

SANDRA: Kinda tough for new kids to fit in. So sometimes they do all sorts of things, just to get attention.

ERIN: What are you trying to tell me about Heather?

SANDRA: Well, the kids think she's—strange.

ERIN: Heather is not strange.

SANDRA: Hey, I'm just trying to forewarn you—before those interfering teachers do. Anyways, Jennifer says Heather tells them, she has a regular captive little audience, about—well, about things she hears—voices that whisper to her. Organ music?

ERIN: Heather is a very imaginative child. She's grown up alone. She talks to her animals. Makes up stories—

SANDRA: Some of them are pretty scary from what I hear. First, the kids were really interested.

ERIN: So she embellished them more.

SANDRA: But now, they stopped believing her, and—

ERIN: I'll talk to her.

SANDRA: Didn't know if I should say anything.

ERIN: I'll take care of it. Things are a little rough right now, at the beginning—working, going to school.

SANDRA: And Heather—she stays alone here, nights you go to school?

ACT ONE

ERIN: It's only two nights a week. I'm home by nine.

SANDRA: Wouldn't let my kids home alone—not in this place.

ERIN: I really do have to get things pushing.

SANDRA: I hear—singing?

ERIN: It's only Heather. She sings to her frog. And I think that's all right.

SANDRA: Sure. Mothers know best.

(Distant singing of Polly Wolly Doodle. *Then* HEATHER *rushes in with groceries, finishing.)*

HEATHER: "Polly Wolly Doodle all the day." Mom, it took me so long, because Polly Wolly wanted to stop at the pond and— *(Notices* SANDRA*)* I'm sorry, I didn't know you had company.

ERIN: This is Mrs Porter, Jennifer's mother.

SANDRA: Hello Heather.

HEATHER: Hello. *(Goes quiet)*

SANDRA: Jennifer's told me all about you. What a bright little girl you are—

HEATHER: She lies.

SANDRA: Jennifer does not lie.

HEATHER: Polly's tired. He wants to go hide in his mud hut. *(Exits upstairs)*

ERIN: I'm sorry—I'll talk to her.

SANDRA: Kids for you.

ERIN: I really need to—

SANDRA: I know. Time for me to put the hog on my table too. Was nice meeting you.

ERIN: Same here. *(Closes door. Calls.)* Heather? I want to talk to you.

HEATHER: *(Coming down stairs)* Polly Wolly and I were going to rest.

ERIN: You weren't very nice to Mrs Porter.

HEATHER: She looks just like Jennifer. Talks like Jennifer and Polly Wolly said he didn't like her and wanted to get away.

ERIN: We'll discuss this later. Right now the table needs to get set. Extra early class tonight.

(ERIN *clears stuff from one end of table. Puts cloth on cleared end.* HEATHER *begins putting on dishes, etc.*)

HEATHER: Is that meat loaf I smell?

ERIN: Yes, and it may be meat loaf for the rest of the week too.

HEATHER: Mom, could I go with you—to your class?

ERIN: No way.

HEATHER: I don't like staying here alone.

ERIN: I don't like it either, but what else can I do? It's only four more weeks.

HEATHER: I could come along—be real quiet.

ERIN: Not allowed. You want a baby sitter?

HEATHER: No, I'm not a baby. Besides, you can't afford it.

ERIN: Say that again.

HEATHER: And again.

ERIN: All you have to do is keep the doors locked, and—

HEATHER: But what if I hear the noises? The music—

ERIN: Stay down here, till I come home. You don't hear them down here, do you?

HEATHER: No.

ACT ONE

ERIN: Turn T V up real loud. Sit with your animals all around you.

HEATHER: Okay.

ERIN: Heather, I don't think you should be telling—well, the things you *think* you hear—to the kids at school.

HEATHER: They like to hear it. Ask every day if I heard anything.

ERIN: Yes, and they tell their parents.

HEATHER: You mean Jennifer's mom.

ERIN: Look, when you're new in school, try to fit in.

HEATHER: *(Throws self on sofa)* I don't want to fit in. I can't fit in—I live in a church—I don't have a father—sisters—brothers— How do I fit in?

ERIN: Poor, poor Heather. *(Pause)* Yeah, you did have lots of friends in Cricket Bay.

HEATHER: And you made me move—from my friends—my school—Grandma.

ERIN: What is wrong with you tonight! We have discussed over and over why we had to move. Life changes. We move on. And there's no way in hell we can ever go back, even if we wanted to, and I certainly don't want to! So, put that in your sweet little head and keep it in that part with things that are true, not in that jumbled space for your made-up stories!

HEATHER: I don't want any supper! *(Runs upstairs)*

ERIN: Heather!!

(Knock on door. Still irritated.)

ERIN: Who's there?

SANDRA: Me—Sandra.

ERIN: *(Hesitates. Opens door.)* Look, I—

SANDRA: Just a quickie. I'm on my second time around the block—but I forgot before—meant to ask you—if you'd like to come—tomorrow night, my house—"Informed Parents Group"?

ERIN: I'm sorry, I don't have time, I'm not interested. I just want to get supper on the table and get to computer class. *(Closing door)*

SANDRA: Sorry I asked.

ERIN: *(Leans against closed door)* I'm sorry too. So sorry about having to be sorry about everything. But I'm in charge of my life now, and I'm not going to do what everyone else thinks I should do. *(Beats fist on door. Turns quickly, shouting.)* Heather! I will give you two minutes to get down here for supper. I will give you one minute to apologize for your behavior—and I will take one half minute to tell you that things are going to be different around here, and that I'm in charge. Do you understand, I am in charge!

(End Scene Two)

Scene Three

(Later that evening. ERIN has returned from class, taking her coat off, putting books away. Intermittent sounds of rain.)

HEATHER: It was really scary tonight, Mom. Scariest it's ever been. I kept hearing those screams.

ERIN: Those high-pitched screams are from the bats.

HEATHER: In our belfry? I don't think so.

ERIN: I'm tired. My brain is overflowing. Just let me reconnect to the real world.

HEATHER: *(Following, using her sense of drama)* Real world? No such thing. There are lots of worlds, Mom. Worlds we can't see—can't explain. And sometimes, there's secret doors to get into them—like your computer. A whole different world in there, and you need the right key to enter.

ERIN: Heather, please—

HEATHER: *(Pause)* Somebody came to the door.

ERIN: What! You didn't open it, did you?

HEATHER: No way. I don't open to nobody. You trained me right. The wind was howling—it was raining—

ERIN: Enough. Thanks for going it alone again. Tell you what, this Saturday, we'll go rummaging—for stuffed animals.

HEATHER: *(Overly dramatic)* No more, please. I can't talk to all those I have now.

ERIN: T V not on?

HEATHER: I didn't want to tell you, not till you got back in the "real" world.

ERIN: Tell me—

HEATHER: I don't know—set was okay. I was watching *Alien Worlds*, when this knocking at the door came— All of a sudden, T V, just popped off.

ERIN: Hitting didn't bring it back?

HEATHER: Nope. Missed the end too.

ERIN: You've seen that ending a hundred times.

HEATHER: But, it's the best part.

ERIN: Dishes done?

HEATHER: Yes. And homework. But I didn't put my clothes out for tomorrow.

ERIN: Why not?

HEATHER: Because I couldn't go upstairs. I couldn't. The organ was playing—

ERIN: All right. You've had a rough enough night. I'll get you up a few minutes early. But I want you to go up there right now, and get ready for bed.

HEATHER: Alone?

ERIN: Yes, alone. I have to practice what I learned tonight, before it evaporates from my dissolving brain cells.

HEATHER: When can I talk to you, tell you about—

ERIN: Saturday. We'll spend all day Saturday— shopping, lunch at the mall, and—

(There's a knock on the door.)

HEATHER: It's the same knock. *(Overly dramatic)* Don't let them in, Mom. Whoever it is, don't let them in.

ERIN: I don't know who it is. *(Pause)* Who's there?

JERICO: My name is Jerico. You don't know me, but I'd like to talk to you, for just a minute.

HEATHER: Don't open the door, Mom.

ERIN: Sorry, I don't open my door to strangers.

JERICO: I don't blame you, Ma'm. But I'm not really a stranger— You see, I used to preach in this church—

ERIN: Well, it's no longer a church. People live here now.

JERICO: I know. They said you were having trouble with the furnace. I can fix it for you.

ERIN: I don't use the furnace. Will you please, just leave.

JERICO: There's this little lever behind the boiler, if it's not set right, blower doesn't kick in. If you let me down there, would just take a minute—

ERIN: We use a wood stove, thank you.

ACT ONE 17

JERICO: Once it gets winter, you'll need that furnace, and somebody's going to charge you an arm and leg to fix it. I'll do it for free.

ERIN: Well—come back Saturday. In daylight.

JERICO: Can't. Leaving tomorrow morning.

ERIN: You can leave right now too.

JERICO: Look Ma'm, you don't even have to let me in, just open the door a crack, so I can see inside my church once more. Would mean a lot to me.

ERIN: *(Pause. Deep breath.)* All right. One second is all you get. *(Opens door slightly, chain still holding it secure)*

HEATHER: Mom—

ERIN: Take your look, and leave.

JERICO: Thank you ever so much. Sure looks different… I couldn't persuade you—

ERIN: My husband's upstairs.

JERICO: I could fix that furnace real quick, be gone before you know it.

ERIN: *(Motions HEATHER to get out of sight. Slowly opens door.)* All right. One minute. And you better know the way to the basement.

JERICO: *(Enters and stands transfixed. He wears jeans, colorful shirt, jean jacket, and one or two indications of his Indian heritage. His voice is powerful and penetrating. A preacher's voice, but not a preaching tone.)* Praise the Lord! It is still a blessed, blessed place.

ERIN: *(Points)* The furnace—

JERICO: Got a flashlight? Dark down there behind that boiler.

HEATHER: *(Comes out from behind sofa)* I was using it, Mom, when the T V broke.

JERICO: Hi.

HEATHER: Hi.

JERICO: I fix T Vs too.

ERIN: My husband—

JERICO: Ma'm, I know all about you two. And I know you don't have a husband, living here.

ERIN: How—

JERICO: I still know people in town. They tell me things.

ERIN: I may not have a husband, but I do have a shotgun. So you better fix that furnace, and leave quick as you can.

JERICO: Be back in two minutes. *(Takes flashlight. Exits through basement doorway.)*

HEATHER: You're always telling me not to let strangers in.

ERIN: When *you* are alone.

HEATHER: You shouldn't have let him in.

ERIN: I know... Maybe I'm so desperate about money—somebody says they'll fix something for nothing, and—

HEATHER: You forget all the rules.

ERIN: I don't know why I did it... Maybe his voice. Something about his voice—made me trust him. And I don't trust too many people.

HEATHER: We don't even have a phone—

ERIN: Or a working furnace—or T V. And who knows what happened to the computer. *(Collapses on sofa)*

HEATHER: And we don't have a shotgun either.

ERIN: But, he doesn't know that.

(All of a sudden lights flash and there's a slight explosion.)

ACT ONE 19

ERIN: *(Jumps up)* Oh my god! *(Runs to basement door)* What's happening down there!

HEATHER: A real fixer. Lucky he didn't blow up the whole place.

JERICO: *(Entering doorway, face all sooty)* Just some loose wires, fumes accumulated, backed up—pow! But, she's going. You wanta come down, I'll show you what to do if—

ERIN: You think I'm crazy or something!

JERICO: *(Looks in mirror next to basement door)* Guess I wouldn't want to go down in a dark basement with me either. An old towel maybe?

ERIN: Heather, some wet paper towels.

*(*HEATHER *exits.)*

JERICO: When I used to preach here—clean white shirt, tie—Sundays and weekdays. Thanks. *(Takes towel from* HEATHER, *wipes face)* But, that was a lifetime ago... Now, let's take a look at that broken T V.

ERIN: That's all right. You fixed enough.

HEATHER: But, we need it working, Mom.

JERICO: Just take a minute. *(At back of T V set)* An old timer, with tubes yet. Not many of these still running. Let's see—this tube—sure looks burned out—can generally substitute this one. Should last for awhile, anyway. *(Pulls out tube. Clicks knob. Picture comes on.)* Presto chango! Now you just take this little tube to the T V store, get a replacement, put it in here—

ERIN: No thanks. I'm not mechanical.

JERICO: Ma'm, it doesn't take mechanical.

HEATHER: Show me. I can do it.

JERICO: See—right here. There's this diagram, too. It's a J2 tube. All you do is push it in— Make sure the set's off.

HEATHER: I can do that. Thanks a lot.

ERIN: How would you like a cup of coffee?

JERICO: You must be reading my mind.

ERIN: —and a piece of apple pie?

JERICO: Homemade?

ERIN: By Thrift Shop Bakeries.

JERICO: Still wouldn't turn it down. *(Walks about)* You know, I used to make apple pies, from the russet apples, tree behind the storage shed. Apple cider too.

ERIN: You really did live here then.

JERICO: I exalted in being here.

HEATHER: Why'd you go away then?

JERICO: Because—circumstances. Misunderstandings.

ERIN: I'll get your food. *(Exits to kitchen)*

HEATHER: Mom's computer's broke too. Polly Wolly and I—

JERICO: Well, let's have a look while we're waiting.

HEATHER: Careful, it's rented.

JERICO: *(Turns it on. Scrambled screen. Passes hands over monitor as if to sense through his hands.)* Hmmm. Any magnets around? I feel strange pullings.

HEATHER: Polly Wolly—he has magnets in his hands. Helps him hop.

JERICO: Maybe. But magnets can screw up computers real good.

HEATHER: How?

ACT ONE 21

JERICO: Well, there's forces on this earth—forces we can't see, that react on things. React on people too. And strange things happen, and we don't always know why. But there's a reason for everything that happens… Now, take Polly Wolly away. *(Does a few clicks. Clear screen comes up.)*

HEATHER: Hey, it works.

JERICO: So it does. The other secret is hitting the right keys. One mistaken key—whole series of problems. (ERIN *enters with tray. Stops and listens.)* But the beauty of a computer—you can always turn it off. Life—can't do that. Oh, you can try, but the past is always there. Clings to you—like a magnet.

ERIN: Here's the coffee, pie, and I had some leftover meatloaf, so I made you a sandwich. *(Sets food on coffee table)*

HEATHER: It works, Mom. Polly Wolly's magnets— made the computer go all scrambly.

ERIN: Both of you keep away from it then.

JERICO: Thank you, Ma'm. *(Folds hands)* Thank you Lord, for bringing me back to this very special place, and these very special people.

HEATHER: Why did you come back here?

JERICO: *(Sits and begins eating)* Don't know if I can answer that exactly… But I did come back looking for work—and maybe some answers. Only, nobody's hiring, and the answers aren't ready yet.

HEATHER: I didn't want to come here.

ERIN: Heather—past your bed time.

HEATHER: I just wanta ask Jerico something else. Jerico—uh, what's your last name, or should I call you "Reverend Jerico"?

ERIN: Heather—

JERICO: It's okay, Ma'm. Your name has a lot to do with who you are. I used to be, "Reverend Jerico Shrader". Now, I'm just plain Jerico Redbird.

HEATHER: Redbird?

JERICO: My father's name. He was a Chippewa Indian. Shrader was my mother's name. She raised me—off the reservation. *(Pause)* Anyway, now I'm back to Jerico Redbird. And I like my name and who I am.

ERIN: All right, Heather.

HEATHER: Just one more question. When you lived here—did you ever hear organ music at night?

JERICO: Organ music? Don't remember. Heard lots of things at night. I still do. Not always sounds—but, well, things in the air. I pick them up. Part of my heritage, I guess.

HEATHER: I hear things—lots of things, in my head. I always have.

ERIN: Heather, brush your teeth please.

(HEATHER *exits to bathroom.*)

ERIN: Heather's supersensitive.

JERICO: I could tell.

ERIN: They say children grow out of it. Just part of the childhood imagination.

JERICO: Is it?

ERIN: Way it was explained to me. Their dolls, stuffed animals, pets—they hear them talking, and the child talks back.

(HEATHER *stands in bathroom doorway, brushing teeth, listening.*)

JERICO: When I was young, I talked to trees—the sun—the moon. My father never thought it strange.

ACT ONE 23

HEATHER: *(Entering, still holding brush)* I never heard trees talk. I'll have to listen, tomorrow.

ERIN: Heather, it's past nine-thirty.

JERICO: I'll be leaving shortly—Ma'm?

ERIN: Erin.

JERICO: Nice Irish name. Nice Irish eyes.

HEATHER: You like meatloaf sandwiches?

JERICO: Enjoying every morsel. The fine company—and this special, special place.

HEATHER: Maybe I'll take the magnets out of Polly Wolly's hands.

JERICO: Don't mutilate him, child. People are made different. Don't try to make him like everyone else. Each of us is unique, in our own way. Maybe he needs magnets. Maybe that makes him a special breed of frog.

HEATHER: Like you and I are a special breed of people, because we hear things in our head.

JERICO: Maybe. But, don't always think "special", `cause sometimes there's simple explanations. Like— well, let me tell you an example. There was this woman, kept hearing songs playing in her head—most drove her crazy. Had all kinds of tests—and you know what one doctor finally found? Fillings in her teeth were acting as a radio receptor. So, she was picking up radio stations through her teeth.

HEATHER: Really? I don't have fillings in my teeth.

ERIN: Well you're going to if you don't finish brushing right now.

HEATHER: All done. *(Picks up Polly Wolly)* Goodnight Jerico Redbird. Thanks for fixing all the stuff. And for telling me those other things, too.

JERICO: Good night, Heather. Pleasant dreams. And may the Lord watch over you.

(HEATHER *hurriedly puts toothbrush in bathroom, exits upstairs, almost skipping.*)

ERIN: We're not any religion, so—

JERICO: Doesn't matter to the Lord. He watches over all of us anyways.

ERIN: It's getting late. *(Picks up dishes)* Thanks again.

JERICO: *(Rises)* Ma'm—I don't know how to ask this, but, well, I don't have a place to stay for the night.

ERIN: That's not my problem, is it.

JERICO: I know. But that little shed—I used to live in there—after the pastor's house burned. Maybe I could sleep in there, just for this night.

ERIN: Sleep in the shed?

JERICO: I'd really appreciate it. Still raining out there.

ERIN: *(Flustered)* I don't even know what's in there. Realty people just opened and shut the door. I wouldn't even know where the key is.

JERICO: Used to be kept— *(Feels above door jamb)* Yep, still here.

ERIN: *(Pause)* I can't—

JERICO: It's all right. I'll sleep across the street—in the park. I've slept in rain before. No problem.

ERIN: *(Pause)* All right. One night only!

JERICO: You're a kind lady. I just wish you weren't so afraid of everything. I pick that up very strongly.

ERIN: You have bedding?

JERICO: Backpack's outside. Travel light these days.

ERIN: This is just for tonight, understand.

ACT ONE

JERICO: I'll be gone in the morning, like the moon that has vanished behind the cloud, maybe returning when you least expect it.

ERIN: I won't be expecting it.

JERICO: Erin, this place—it's not the same. I've been picking up bad vibrations. People were telling me about the group that lived here before. You might want a special blessing on this building.

ERIN: No blessings!

JERICO: Sorry, just trying to help, best way I know how.

ERIN: You've helped enough. Good night.

JERICO: Bless you.

ERIN: Good night! And you'd better be gone by morning!

(JERICO *leaves.* ERIN *locks door, props chair. Turns on computer, T V.*)

HEATHER: *(Calling softly)* Mom?

ERIN: What now?

HEATHER: *(Standing in doorway in long white nightgown)* Is he gone—the Redbird man?

ERIN: Yes.

HEATHER: Doesn't feel like he's gone.

ERIN: Well, he's staying the night, in the shed.

HEATHER: The shed?

ERIN: He needed a place to sleep.

HEATHER: Oh. You know, it was kinda nice, having him here. Fixing stuff. He talked nice too. Knows things. Things none of us know... Maybe he could fix your car.

ERIN: It runs.

HEATHER: It rattles.

ERIN: For you every sound is magnified a hundred times. I hardly hear it anymore.

HEATHER: Wait—vibrations. In the floor. Is the furnace running?

ERIN: I guess it is now—till we run out of oil anyway. Let's go up to bed.

HEATHER: It was warm here before. Now, there's a real cold chill—

ERIN: *(Shouting)* Enough already! Give me one night of peace, please. And stop making this place into a house of horror!

(They exit. Pause. Then a sound from deep in the basement begins as a small rumble. The bookcases shake. The animals tremble and fall and vases begin to topple. Then articles begin flying about. The T V blares, computer goes crazy. Bizarre organ music plays in the distance.)

(End Scene Three)

Scene Four

(The next evening. Bookcases are upright. Vases are back. Stuffed animals in jumbled pile. ERIN *has been folding laundry; now she is standing, talking to* JERICO.*)*

ERIN: I thought you left—for good.

JERICO: Just came back one more time—see that the furnace was still running okay.

ERIN: You checked it out this morning—before you left. Remember?

JERICO: I know, but I just wanted to make sure, and—

ERIN: Well, I'm still upset about it. The whole episode.

JERICO: I told you, the furnace, it backfired.

ERIN: Scaring the hell out of Heather and me.

JERICO: Because it hadn't been used, all this gunk accumulated—I tell you what, I'll get some stuff at the hardware store, work on it tomorrow—

ERIN: Tomorrow? One night. You were given only one night.

JERICO: I know. But, today, I got a job.

ERIN: Where?

JERICO: Whambos. That fast food place. Clean up and stuff. I get food too.

ERIN: Well, if that's your ambition in life.

JERICO: Not really. But, it'll do for now. Only—I still need a place to stay.

ERIN: Sorry, not here.

JERICO: Just hear me out. That shed—would do me for a couple of months, till it got real cold. Then I'd be on my way. Wouldn't bother you—for food, anything. Might even bring you some. *(Leans against dining table. Leg wobbles.)*

ERIN: I don't need any extra problems.

JERICO: *(Takes out screwdriver on Swiss Army knife. Begins tightening screws on table leg as he talks.)* Extra help? This place could sure use some. I could paint the whole outside for you. Really enjoy doing that. Fixing up my old church.

ERIN: It is not a church.

JERICO: Okay, we'll unmake it out of a church. Take off that shaky belfry. Redo the windows.

ERIN: I don't want anybody else around here.

JERICO: Wouldn't even need to come into the house. Wash up at Whambos—

ERIN: I have a little girl.

JERICO: I would never harm—I swear it, on a stack of Bibles.

ERIN: *(Pause)* There's too much I don't know about you.

JERICO: Okay, what would you like to know? *(Sits)*

ERIN: Well—why did you leave this church? Why are you back?

JERICO: Why did I leave.

(Pause)

ERIN: You don't have to—

JERICO: No, it's okay. It's just that I want to make sure I tell it right. Might mean the difference between you letting me stay here or not.

ERIN: Wait—there's still some warm coffee. *(Exits to kitchen with laundry basket)*

JERICO: My beautiful, beautiful church... *(Extends hands, walks about, sensing things)* The evil's still here. *(Clasps hands in prayer)*

ERIN: *(Returns with tray. Presentational style.)* And tonight we have—Thrift Shop Bakeries apple cake.

JERICO: Some day I'm going to show you how very easy it is to make russet apple pie.

ERIN: Don't count your apples, till I hear your story.

JERICO: *(Sits and begins eating)* Well, I told you my father, Thunder Horse, was Chippewa Indian. As council member of the Native American Church he traveled all over the country to their meetings. Pow wows. Summers, my mother let me go along. I'd sit on the fringes, not quite understanding. But during the religious ceremonies, that's when I was one with them. The chanting, dancing, drums, even Christian symbols. And sometimes peyote buttons were passed around...

One night, my father let me try peyote. The visions were spectacular—mystical… *(Pauses. Eats.)* Sure good apple cake. *(Pause)* That was the last summer I went with my father—he died that fall. Mama Shrader, she stripped everything Indian away. I felt vacant—lost. Not belonging anywhere…

ERIN: I know that feeling.

JERICO: *(Rises. Enacting the memory.)* One night, in my teens, I went to a Pentecostal church meeting. There was shouting. Clapping. Chantlike songs. A real communal feeling, vibrating memories of those childhood Indian gatherings. I joined in. Was baptized in the Holy Spirit. And went all the way to being a preacher… My very first parish was this church.

ERIN: I see.

JERICO: The Church of the Holy Ghost… They closed it down after I left and I heard a pretty wild group moved in here, and—

ERIN: I don't want to know—just about you.

JERICO: Fair enough. Oh, I was the most zealous preacher you ever did see. Wanting everyone to envision God as I did. So, I formed this young people's group. We met in the woods, around a campfire. Prayed. Sang. Still wasn't reaching them. Needed something more… *(Stops as painful memory returns)*

ERIN: If it's too painful—

JERICO: Thought it was gone… Anyway, I told them about peyote—the visions. How it had brought me closer to God. And if they prayed real hard, it could happen for them too, without peyote. They wanted to see what it looked like… So I brought some, next meeting, inside this church. *(Pause)* Sonny, that was his name, stole some, ate some, while we were all praying… There was a cry of the hound that rose up from the depths of this building. Sonny started yelling, running up the stairs, as if demons were released and pursuing him.

ERIN: Oh no.

JERICO: I followed. Couldn't catch him. The bell started ringing. Sonny jumped—fell—off the belfry. I tried to stop him, but something physically grabbed me, held me back. *(Stops)* Sonny died. They tried to blame it on the peyote. Couldn't prove it. I knew it was something else pushed him off that belfry… I went to prison. Possession of illegal drugs. Contributing to the delinquency of minors.

ERIN: So you were in prison.

JERICO: I don't keep it secret.

ERIN: How long?

JERICO: Long enough to lose all my faith—and find it again. But, in an entirely different way. I had time there to meditate, think, read. Found my way back even deeper and stronger.

ERIN: You still have it?

JERICO: Oh yes. Explodes from my hands sometimes.

ERIN: And after prison?

JERICO: Been out about a year. Traveling. Doing odd jobs. Then, decided I needed to start over. So, I came back here.

ERIN: All this soul searching and you end up at Whambos?

JERICO: All this soul searching, and I'm back at my church.

ERIN: This not a church anymore!

JERICO: Sorry. Figuratively speaking.

ACT ONE

ERIN: No. You're a strong believer and I don't know if I'm strong enough to tune you out.

JERICO: I promise I won't—

ERIN: Heather and I don't need anybody else trying to save us.

JERICO: I've given up trying to change people. Save them. I only offer help. Every one needs that.

ERIN: There it is—that savior tone.

JERICO: Savior? All I'm asking is a place to stay—in return for fixing up this building. Nothing else implied or intended.

ERIN: *(Pause)* All right. We'll try it out, one week at a time. If it doesn't work—I've taken classes, had counseling—learned to speak out.

JERICO: You've learned assertiveness.

ERIN: Which my mother never taught me.

JERICO: How come there aren't any classes for compassion? If assertiveness can be taught, why not compassion?

ERIN: I warned you, no sermons.

JERICO: Don't quite say the right things, do I.

ERIN: I know exactly what you're saying…I went through all the therapy I need. Learned how to control my head, body—emotions. But none of that means a damn thing if I can't put food on the table.
You can know all the answers—right emotions—but unless you can earn a living, you're never in charge of your life. I can earn a paycheck. That's what helps me survive. This paycheck keeps my daughter and myself clothed, fed, and housed. And, in order to earn this paycheck, I need a skill, a marketable skill. And that has nothing to do with knowing how to be assertive, compassionate, and all those other abstract things.

I can type. I can use a computer. And you can clean up the shit at some fast food place. And that's what keeps us going. And don't you and all those other people with P h Ds dangling after their names try to tell me any different!

JERICO: *(Claps)* Bravo!

ERIN: *(Embarrassed)* Sorry, I got carried away a little.

JERICO: You should do it more often.

ERIN: Never anybody around to hear me.

JERICO: Then do it for yourself. Maybe you're the only one who needs to hear.

ERIN: Maybe...

HEATHER: *(Cries from upstairs)* No! No!

JERICO: What's going on?

ERIN: Heather, she has nightmares.

JERICO: Nightmares?

ERIN: Since moving here.

HEATHER: Keep away from me! Keep away!

JERICO: Doesn't sound like nightmares to me.

ERIN: I'll deal with this, in my own way.

HEATHER: Help me! Somebody help me!

JERICO: Those aren't nightmares. That child needs help.

ERIN: Will you please—just leave!

HEATHER: *(Running down the stairs.)* Mommy—Mommy!! The man—he came after me again!

ERIN: *(Holding her)* It's all right, honey. Just another bad dream.

HEATHER: It wasn't a dream this time. The room got all cold and shivery—a blue light came. Then all of a

ACT ONE 33

sudden, he was—standing right by my bed. *(Shudders and cries)*

ERIN: Calm down, Heather. Just calm down now.

JERICO: What did this man look like?

ERIN: I'll take care of this.

HEATHER: Let Jerico help—he fixes things.

JERICO: Can you describe the man.

HEATHER: I've seen him before—in my dreams. But never like tonight. Not right beside my bed.

ERIN: It's okay. It's over now.

HEATHER: *(Continuing)* He—he had dark black hair. Evil looking eyes—a pointy beard, and— *(Stops as if not wanting to remember)*

JERICO: That all?

HEATHER: Nooo. On his hand, a painted snake—a snake that went all the way up his arm. And he—and he— *(Hand over mouth)* I'm going to be sick. *(Rushes to bathroom)*

ERIN: Oh my god—oh my god! *(Collapses on sofa)*

JERICO: Who is this man?

ERIN: *(To herself)* He always said he'd get her. Screamed it at me—

JERICO: Who?

ERIN: I can't tell you—or her. Can't even think about it… *(Gets up)* I'm going to help Heather.

JERICO: *(Stops her)* You have to let me help you.

ERIN: Just leave. Leave us alone!

JERICO: There's something evil here. Something trying to get Heather. Believe me, I know about such things.

ERIN: You know nothing! And I am not going to stand here and listen to your religious garbage. Get out, right now!

HEATHER: *(Out of bathroom. Sits in recliner.)* I'm okay now. I threw up all the bad stuff.

ERIN: Just another terrible dream, honey.

HEATHER: No, not this time. He said he was coming to get me. And— *(Pauses. Breathing heavily.)* He said—he was going to get you too. He said— *(The horror of it makes her stop. Faints slowly to floor)*

ERIN: *(Falls apart)* Noooo—he can't do this.

JERICO: She's in shock—fainted. I'll put her on the couch.

ERIN: *(Trembling)* Should I get a doctor? We don't have a phone—

JERICO: *(Covers* HEATHER *with blankets)* Wait a bit. Keep her warm, quiet. *(Makes sign of cross over her, then lays hands on her forehead)* She's resting now.

ERIN: *(In her own sphere of remembering. Sobbing.)* I can't go through it again. I can't... I can't even think about him without— *(Starts gagging)*

JERICO: Who is this man?

ERIN: You don't need to know.

JERICO: I need to know whoever, whatever it is you're fighting. Who is he?

ERIN: *(Sobbing)* He's—he's—

JERICO: Let it out—

ERIN: *(Screams out)* The devil who raped me! Tried to kill me—

JERICO: God in heaven. Is he still alive?

ERIN: I don't know. They sent him to prison. I testified.

ACT ONE

JERICO: It must be him.

ERIN: How? He's locked up.

JERICO: Doesn't matter. They can do their work anywhere. Especially from behind bars.

ERIN: Heather was born—after the rape.

JERICO: His child. He's trying to get at his child.

ERIN: *(Goes to* HEATHER, *backing away from any more revealing)* She's breathing normal. I think she'll be okay. I don't want doctors. I can't tell them—and if they ask her—they might take her away from me again.

JERICO: *(Comes to* ERIN*)* Do you want to tell me.

ERIN: I can't. I can't talk about it. I'm so close to cracking up— *(Stops)* Heather needs me. My mother can't take care of her anymore. And there's nobody to take care of me—

JERICO: *(Holds her. She rests head on his shoulders.)* Please, let me help you. Take care of you both.

HEATHER: *(Half asleep. Not in terrified tones as before.)* Mommy—don't let that man take me away. Don't…

JERICO: *(Goes to her. Gently.)* We're not going to let anybody take you away. We're going to fight whoever, whatever it is. And we're going to win.

HEATHER: *(Jumps up, letting out terrified scream)* He's down here now! Don't let him get me! *(Pulls blanket around herself to hide)*

(A chill sweeps through the room. A faint blue light—then evil laughter.)

ERIN: *(Shelters* HEATHER *with her body. Strongly.)* Nobody's going to get you. Nobody!

JERICO: *(Rises and begins singing to drown out sounds As laughter gets louder, he sings louder and stronger.)* Amazing grace, how the sweet the sound

That saved a wretch like me!
I once was lost, but now am found
Was blind, but now I see.

(JERICO *walks about room, arms upraised. Lights begin dimming.*)

JERICO: Through many dangers, toils, and snares—
I have already come...

(Curtain)

END ACT ONE

ACT TWO

Scene One

(Evening. One week later. Bookshelves are empty. Gothic window is draped over, paint cloths about. ERIN *is busying about getting ready for class.* HEATHER *sits, dangling Polly Wolly at her feet.)*

HEATHER: I told you I don't feel well, Mom.

ERIN: Just rest—on the sofa, till I get back.

HEATHER: But—

ERIN: Please—don't upset me, I have to do well on this test.

HEATHER: But I can't sleep nights anymore.

ERIN: Not now! When I come home— Can you wait `til then?

HEATHER: I'll have to.

ERIN: Thanks.

HEATHER: When's Jerico through work?

ERIN: I don't know if it's his late night or not.

HEATHER: He was going to find out—

(There's frantic pounding on the door.)

SANDRA: Erin! Erin! Let me in!!

ERIN: *(Unlocks door as pounding continues)* Oh my god, what happened—

SANDRA: *(Rushes in, near hysteria, mouth bleeding, carrying stuffed tote bag)* He beat me—that son of a bitch! Came home and beat the crap out of me.

ERIN: Who?

SANDRA: *(Circles room angrily)* The shit—my husband! I'm moving out, tomorrow. Nobody's gonna do this to me.

ERIN: Sit down.

SANDRA: I need a place to stay—just for tonight.

ERIN: Here?

SANDRA: He'll look every place in town. But he'd never think of coming here. Please—

ERIN: Sure—it's okay. But, I have to go to class.

HEATHER: Let her stay, Mom.

SANDRA: I just ran out. Didn't know where I was going—then I saw your church. I didn't plan—just came here.

ERIN: Why didn't you go to the police?

SANDRA: Police? Hah! His drinking buddies. Sits with them at Barney's Tap, boozing, talking down women— or talking up the ones they seduce. I hate all men! *(Collapses in heap on sofa. Takes can of cold beer from bag, puts on her jaw.)*

ERIN: *(Hands her towel from back of chair)* You want a doctor?

SANDRA: No! God no!

ERIN: Pills? I have some—for the terrible times.

SANDRA: Noooo—I just want this day to go away— forever.

ERIN: I have to leave, for class. It's a test night. Will you be okay? Heather will be here.

ACT TWO

SANDRA: I'll be okay. Just don't open the door, to nobody. *(Familiar knock on door)* Don't answer it!!

ERIN: It's only Jerico.

HEATHER: *(Brightening)* It is his early night.

ERIN: *(Opens door)* Hi, Jerico. I was just leaving.

JERICO: I ran over quick with some leftovers. Chicken—dried french fries. And who likes melted ice cream? The machine went down and— *(Notices* SANDRA*)* Sorry, I didn't know someone was here.

ERIN: A neighbor—friend. She's staying the night.

JERICO: Her name Sandra?

ERIN: Yes—why?

JERICO: Some guy was running down the road screaming like crazy, "Sandra! Sandra!!"

SANDRA: *(Sits up)* You son of a bitch—if you tell him I'm here—

JERICO: Your husband? He do that to you?

SANDRA: None of your damn business. I don't need you prying into my affairs.

JERICO: I was only—

SANDRA: I know all about you. My nephew was in your "youth group". And—

ERIN: That's enough! Just calm down now.

SANDRA: *(Holds jaw in pain)* God, I hope he didn't break it. *(Huddles under blanket, moaning)*

HEATHER: Mom, is she going to be okay?

SANDRA: Any whiskey? I need something more potent. Beer was all I could grab.

ERIN: I don't keep liquor around anymore.

SANDRA: Times like this I gotta come to a dry church.

JERICO: You came to some beautiful people who have problems of their own. Don't add to them.

SANDRA: *(Opens can of beer, as she drinks.)* I didn't come for your preaching! You men are all alike. Rulers of the world! Keeping women as your slaves. We should worship at your feet, and—

ERIN: That's enough! Heather, get my coat. I need to leave.

HEATHER: Okay. *(Exits up stairs)*

ERIN: You just calm down now. I'll be home by nine, earlier if I can. We'll talk then. Kinda watch it with the beer, okay?

SANDRA: Is "he" staying here?

JERICO: No Ma'm. I stay in my own place, and—

ERIN: We have our own arrangement. It works out. I'll just put this food away quick. *(Exits to kitchen)*

SANDRA: I don't know why you came back here. Didn't prison teach you anything?

JERICO: Many, many things.

HEATHER: *(Coming down stairs)* Here's your coat and purse, Mom.

JERICO: She's putting food away.

HEATHER: *(Secretively)* Jerico, what if it happens again tonight?

JERICO: We're not going to talk about it—right now.

HEATHER: Okay.

ERIN: *(Returning)* You can watch T V—movie only.

HEATHER: I don't like T V anymore.

ERIN: Don't have time—I'm leaving. Lock up after me.

JERICO: I'll walk you to your car. Then maybe try to get a good night's sleep.

ACT TWO

ERIN: You don't have to get up at the crack of dawn each day to paint this place, you know.

JERICO: Has to get done.

(Both are gone. HEATHER *locks door.)*

HEATHER: *(Sits on floor. Talking to Polly Wolly.)* What if he comes to my bed again tonight. He said he wasn't going to leave me alone. He was going to keep coming—and coming—

SANDRA: *(Half sleeping)* Hmmm—what did you say?

HEATHER: Nothing… But I wouldn't stay here tonight if I was you. There's bad bad things happening in this place. You don't want to know about the bad things that go on here.

SANDRA: *(Still groggy)* Does he bother you honey?

HEATHER: Every night. Every night he comes to my bed—and—

SANDRA: And what?

HEATHER: Does bad things.

SANDRA: *(Sits up. Alert)* That son of a bitch. That son of a bitch Jerico.

HEATHER: No—not Jerico. He's my friend.

SANDRA: Then who's bothering you?

HEATHER: I don't know. He's—he's a man—with evil eyes—and a snake running up his arm.

SANDRA: A snake?

HEATHER: Grandma said to watch out for a man with a snake on his arm.

SANDRA: I don't get this. *(Pause)* You're making this stuff up, aren't you. Just some more of those crazy stories you keep making up. *(Lays back down)*

HEATHER: *(Sits at other end of sofa, begins to cry)* Nobody believes me.

SANDRA: *(Sits up, takes* HEATHER's *hand. Talks to her as an adult.)* It's okay. We all have our demons inside of us. Some we can't fight while we're awake—so we fight them when we sleep. Or fight them in the bottle. But you always gotta keep fighting them. Else they overtake you.

HEATHER: *(Pulls away)* I don't want to fight him anymore. Pretty soon—some night—I'm going to just go away with him, because—because—he says he'll kill Mom if I don't. And he describes how he'll do it. He— He—

SANDRA: *(Gets up, walks away, hands over ears)* I don't want to hear it! I don't want to hear any more how some man is going to torture some woman.

HEATHER: What can I do about it? *(Sits on floor)*

SANDRA: *(Bends to her. Almost admonishing.)* Listen honey, this is what these terrible imaginations can do to you. Get into your head, turn things all around—till you don't know what is real or not anymore. You have to believe—that when you're awake—that's real! And when you're asleep—that's not.

HEATHER: He is real, yet he isn't. Like he's a ghost, yet he's not. Whatever he is—he's bad—real bad. *(Begins sobbing)*

SANDRA: What does your mom say about this?

HEATHER: I can't tell her—some parts.

SANDRA: Well—

HEATHER: I shouldn't have told you. But I had to tell somebody.

(There's a fierce pounding on the door.)

MALE VOICE: Sandra! Sandra!!

ACT TWO

SANDRA: *(Jumps up. Takes* HEATHER *and moves away from door.)* It's him! Keep still. Don't say anything!!

(Pounding and calling continues at each boarded up window.)

JERICO: *(Loudly from outside)* What's going on out here? This is a church! *(Muffled replies)* Now you just get out of here!

HEATHER: We're lucky to have Jerico around. He's not afraid of anybody.

SANDRA: Well, you just be careful of him.

HEATHER: Why?

SANDRA: *(Walks and drinks as she talks)* You just be careful of all men. Don't ever believe anything they tell you. They try to touch you—lay one little finger on you—you scream bloody murder and run tell your mother, anybody.

HEATHER: I'm only scared of this one man, who comes in the night.

SANDRA: *(Back to lying on sofa)* I'm going to rest now, okay. Maybe when I wake up this pain and my nightmare will be over. Maybe yours will be too.

HEATHER: I'll just sit here. *(Sits in recliner)*

SANDRA: T V won't bother me.

HEATHER: I don't watch T V anymore. He—he gets into the T V—and then he even talks to me from there.

SANDRA: *(Already dozing)* Well just do something, `til your mom gets back.

HEATHER: She only has two more weeks of class.

SANDRA: That's nice. *(Dozes off)*

HEATHER: *(Tenses. Looks about.)* The music. Do you hear the music, Sandra? Mom never hears it. Do you hear it?

SANDRA: Hmmmm.

HEATHER: *(Holding Polly Wolly. Talking rapidly.)* Jerico says he hears it. He's supersensitive. So am I. We see and hear things other people don't. He says it's like we're a conduit wire between two worlds—picking up different things. Only, I don't know how to shut them off. Jerico says singing helps. Blocks the waves or something... He sings hymns. I don't know any. *(Stands up, puts hands over ears, then starts singing to drown out whatever she is hearing as she walks about the room.)*
Oh I went down south for to see my gal
Singing Polly Wolly Doodle all the day—
(Repeating)
Polly Wolly Doodle all the day
Polly Wolly Doodle all the day—
I hope you don't mind me singing. That's the only way I can drown everything out. *(Continues)*
Fare thee well—Fare thee well
Fare thee well to Cricket Bay—

(Stops. Silence. A blue light comes up, quivering over everything.)

HEATHER: Oh no, it's starting again. Don't! Don't let it happen tonight! I'm going to stand here and scream and scream so I can't hear anything else.

(Stands with hands over ears, screaming continuously as evil laughter is heard in background.)

(End Scene One)

Scene Two

(A few hours later. Empty beer cans piled on coffee table. SANDRA is now drinking coffee.)

ACT TWO 45

ERIN: *(Coming down the stairs)* I think she's sleeping now.

SANDRA: Never heard a kid scream like that before. Shocked the shit out of me.

ERIN: It's only been this past week. I'm hoping it will go away, like it came, and my classes will be over, and I'll get that raise—and life will go forward, instead of backwards.

SANDRA: No phone—and I couldn't even go for help. This has been one hell of a night, I tell you. *(Grabs for beer can; it's empty.)*

ERIN: Everything's all right now.

SANDRA: You kidding? That Heather needs help.

ERIN: She'll be okay.

SANDRA: Look, not much scares this toughie. But tonight, weird things were going on around here. Those bookcases, they weren't just shakin' by themselves, even if I was half crocked.

ERIN: The furnace—

SANDRA: Crap! That was no furnace. And I heard—other sounds—cold winds. Then that kid screaming. Thought I was in a drunken nightmare.

ERIN: I'm sorry if she upset you.

SANDRA: She's the upset one. Told me about—some man coming to get her. Creeepy.

ERIN: Really. *(Pause)* She's told me that before too. Just—stories.

SANDRA: Who you kidding.

ERIN: I—I can't talk about it. Okay? Don't ask me to.

SANDRA: Sorry, I'm not in much shape to be any kind of support tonight.

ERIN: *(Introspectively)* How is he doing it—

SANDRA: Look, I decided, I'm going to JoJo's, my sister.

ERIN: What?

SANDRA: Sampson's probably sleeping it off by now, so I'm gonna hoof it over to JoJo's. Spend what's left of the night there.

ERIN: Sure. It might be best. *(Gathers beer cans)*

SANDRA: Some advice. Don't let that jailbird preacher talk you into anything. Or try to help you.

ERIN: I'm trying my best not to. *(Exits to kitchen with cans)*

SANDRA: He was sacked out of this church you know.

ERIN: *(Returning)* Yes, he told me.

SANDRA: Tell you why?

ERIN: Yes.

SANDRA: And you still don't worry about Heather?

ERIN: Yes, I worry about Heather. I worry about myself. I worry about so many things… He's painting this place—that's all. Then he's leaving.

SANDRA: Well, it's your crap shoot. *(Getting her things together. Checks self in purse mirror.)* Just hope JoJo lets me in. Usually I phone—

ERIN: Maybe you shouldn't—go out all alone, this late at night.

SANDRA: Pooh—lots of times I jog at midnight. I'm tough. Only, that son of a bitch is tougher.

ERIN: They all are.

SANDRA: Karate. Next on my list. That asshole lays one stinkin finger on me—pow!! Broken bones.

ERIN: They can overpower you with their evil, without even being near you.

ACT TWO

SANDRA: Come on, you seen too many Exorcist movies. That why you moved to a church, get away from all the evils? Hell, there's no place on earth you can hide from it. But by god, you learn to fight, any way you can, even when you can't see it. You fight and fight and fight!

ERIN: And if you're not strong enough—

SANDRA: Then you get help.

ERIN: If you're alone—no one to help—

SANDRA: Hey, this is a great big populated world. You're never alone, always somebody out there. A big supermarket of help—A A, Parents Without Partners— therapy groups—support groups.

ERIN: I've been through most. What's happening here isn't something they can help me with. There's no group for these kinds of things.

SANDRA: Look, I gotta go. But I'll find help for you— someplace.

ERIN: No! I don't want you telling anybody—about tonight.

SANDRA: Who'd believe me.

ERIN: *(Opening door locks)* Be careful out there.

(ERIN *opens door. Sounds of crickets. Looks right and left.*)

ERIN: Coast is clear.

SANDRA: *(Standing in doorway. Looks both ways, then up)* Peaceful out here now... See, way up in that sky— billions and billons of miles away—those tiny blinking stars. They just keep wheeling around, on their own little path, like we don't matter at all. Does anybody even know we're down here.

ERIN: *(Shakes head)* I often wonder...

(ERIN *and* SANDRA*y hug.*)

ERIN: Come back when you can. Soon.

SANDRA: Sooner than you think.

(*Watches after. Then closes and locks door. Picks up saucers. Stops, as though hearing something. Shivers, as if a cold wind were going through, saucers shaking in her hand. All of a sudden the lights blink, bookcases begin shaking.*)

ERIN: (*Puts saucers down*) No! Not any more tonight!

(ERIN *opens door and runs out. Sounds and shaking continue.*)

HEATHER: (*From above, screams out, terrified*) Keep away from me! Keep away!! I won't go with you! I won't!!

(ERIN *and* JERICO *enter hurriedly,* JERICO *still pulling on T-shirt.*)

ERIN: I'm sorry I had to wake you, but I didn't know what else to do. (*Pause*) It's stopped—the shaking—the screaming.

JERICO: Want me to check on Heather?

ERIN: I'll go up. (*She exits.*)

(JERICO *examines bookcases. Shakes them. Extends arms as if trying to pick up vibrations. Walks about room.*)

ERIN: (*Returns*) She's okay. Sorry I woke you, but—

JERICO: I told you, any time.

ERIN: It's been every night this week.

JERICO: You have to tell me more, so I know what I'm dealing with.

ERIN: I can't tell you more, because I don't know any more.

JERICO: She's not making this up.

ERIN: I used to think so.

JERICO: Those bookcases—furnace didn't do that.

ACT TWO

ERIN: Then what? What is it? This building?

JERICO: I'm not sure. But whatever it is—it's angry.

ERIN: It has to be him.

JERICO: The man who raped you?

ERIN: He—he said he would get me, somehow. I still hear him screaming—"The child belongs to me!"

JERICO: When did he say this?

ERIN: In court. On the witness stand... Oh my god, it's all coming back—everything. His face—his words—

JERICO: Let it all come out then. Slowly. Like vomit. You'll feel better after.

ERIN: I can't—

JERICO: Try. Take your time.

ERIN: I carry it with me, every day.

JERICO: Release it then.

ERIN: *(Sits quietly for moment. Then begins breathing heavily. Speaks in short gasps)* I—I was walking home—alone. I heard footsteps, behind me. I went faster. He went faster... *(Stops)*

JERICO: Then what?

ERIN: He—he grabbed me from behind—so tight—I couldn't breathe. A knife—at my throat. I couldn't even scream—make any sound. He put this bag over my head—tied my hands, feet—shoved me into the trunk of his car.

(Pause)

JERICO: Take your time.

ERIN: *(As if there, reliving)* When he took the bag off—I was in this farm building. A concrete room. Women in chains, against the walls, everywhere. He tied me with ropes and he did things to me—horrible things.

Poured liquids in every opening of my body. I finally passed out... When I woke up, it was quiet. My skin still slippery—from the liquids. I rubbed my wrists raw, somehow, slipped out of the ropes. One woman pointed, she couldn't even talk—to a small door in the bottom of the huge locked door, where they shoved food in. I slid through. Ran, naked, bleeding— *(Anguished cries rise up from her depths as she goes into a slight faint.)*

JERICO: Just relax now. It's all over, all cried out.

ERIN: *(Reviving)* They found me. I don't remember that part. Just waking up in a hospital bed and screaming over and over about that place—the women still there.

JERICO: Finish later.

ERIN: It never finishes.

JERICO: Do it now then.

ERIN: ...They caught him. Found the other women too. All dead by then. Starved. Tortured. I was the only one alive to testify. It was months before the trial... *(Pause)* Once I knew I was pregnant, I wanted to tear it out of me. Every memory of that horrible night... *(Different tone)* I went to this clinic. They strapped me to this table. Strong hands holding me down. My body began quivering. This masked doctor's face, coming closer. "We're going to vacuum it out of you—" "No!" I didn't want anything entering my body again.
I let out this terrifying scream, that wailed away into a continuous faraway sound—the faint cry of a newborn baby. I closed my eyes as tight as I could, but all I could see was this beam of light—a pinpoint of brightness piercing through all the deep dark. Every instinct within me clawed to protect this one spark of light, because if I let it go out—everything would become total darkness again. Saving this speck of life was the only hope of saving myself. I screamed and

ACT TWO

screamed and broke loose. And I escaped—just like the time before…

JERICO: *(Takes her hand)* I cry in my heart for everything's that's happened to you.

ERIN: *(Jerks her hand away)* I fought my mother—I fought everybody—to keep this child. I had always wanted a baby and this might be my only chance…I knew I'd never have sex again.

JERICO: I've heard what I need to know.

ERIN: I was on the witness stand. He was in handcuffs. He screamed at me, before they could stop him—"I'll get you, and our bastard child, if it's the last thing I do!" I fainted.

JERICO: It has to be him.

ERIN: *(Calming)* I never regretted saving her. Heather was the most beautiful baby… We moved to another town. Mama couldn't face the people. I had therapy, tried to forget. Years went by. Then, I started having these terrible nightmares. He would come to me—it was like reliving that night over each time. I had to be institutionalized. My mother raised Heather, the two years I was away. After, we lived together, the three of us. Then Mama died. I wanted to make a new start. So we moved here.

JERICO: Thinking you could leave it all behind.

ERIN: They told me in therapy, it was all in my mind, that he couldn't really get to me. I believed them. But now I know, his evil is so strong, he can project it anywhere he wants.

JERICO: There are people who can do more behind bars than outside, because they have time to concentrate their whole being on projecting their evils.

ERIN: You've been there.

JERICO: Yes, and I met his kind.

ERIN: You're probably the only one who can help us then—if anyone can.

JERICO: We're going to use every counterattack known. Do you have a picture of him? *(Up. Contemplates as he walks.)*

ERIN: I burned every scrap.

JERICO: Newspaper photos?

ERIN: The most evil pictures you ever want to see. The dead women. And hundreds of photos of him—all with that depraved smile.

JERICO: I'll go to the library, tomorrow.

ERIN: Let it alone.

JERICO: He's not letting you alone.

ERIN: Or Heather. She's the one I care about.

JERICO: Right now he's only playing mind games. Physically he can't touch you. You have to believe that.

ERIN: And Heather?

JERICO: Children are more susceptible. Somehow he's been able to project his evil spirit out of that prison and into this place—connecting with your child, when she's sleeping, her mind more relaxed. Geneological mind links have been proven.

ERIN: Don't say that. I've disconnected any trace of him from her entirely.

JERICO: What did you tell her about her father?

ERIN: That he's dead. Killed in an auto accident. Only I never knew what my mother told her, those years I was away. Mama had her own phobias.

HEATHER: *(Screams out)* Keep away from me! Keep away!

ACT TWO 53

(ERIN *rushes to go upstairs.* JERICO *stops her.*)

JERICO: Let me.

ERIN: No—

HEATHER: Help me!! Somebody help me!!

ERIN: Go!

(JERICO *runs upstairs.*)

ERIN: *(Low and threatening)* Keep away from her. She doesn't belong to you. She never belonged to you…

(JERICO *carries a sobbing* HEATHER *down the stairs. She goes to* ERIN's *arms.*)

HEATHER: He cut me. See.

ERIN: Oh my god.

JERICO: It's just a scratch.

HEATHER: He—he had a knife. Said he would do more.

JERICO: I'll get some antiseptic. *(Goes to bathroom)*

ERIN: You can sleep down here tonight, on the recliner. Okay? *(Places her on recliner)*

HEATHER: I don't want to live in this place anymore.

ERIN: *(Covers her)* Just rest now. We'll both stay here with you, while you sleep.

HEATHER: He says he's my father. Only he doesn't look like my father's picture at all. And, he has this snake—

ERIN: *(Breaks into singing)*
Oh I went down South, for to see my gal,
Singing Polly Wolly Doodle all the day.
Oh my Heather am a purty little gal—

JERICO: *(Entering)* Some Bactine. It's hard to tell if she scratched herself, or—these things are so difficult.

(ERIN *motions to be still. Continues humming as* JERICO *cleans the scratch.*)

HEATHER: *(Half asleep)* No! Don't cut me again—no!

(HEATHER *squirms away in convulsionlike motions. They hold her down.*)

ERIN: *(Singing faster)* Fare thee well, fare thee well—

JERICO: *(Blessing* HEATHER*)* Peace child—peace.

ERIN: *(Half laughing, half crying)* Me singing—you blessing— What modern voodoo is this!

JERICO: Whatever—she's calmed down.

ERIN: And if it happens again?

JERICO: I'm staying here with both of you—'til this night is over.

ERIN: And tomorrow night—and the next?

JERICO: We're going to start fighting back, every night.

ERIN: How?

JERICO: There's only one way to fight this evil.

ERIN: No religious rituals.

JERICO: You don't have to be here when I do it.

ERIN: I won't go backward, believing in prayer— Some hokus pokus magic cure-all. I've learned to take responsibility for myself, not rely on something out there that doesn't even exist.

JERICO: It exists all right. Believe me. I've witnessed things that would convince the greatest unbeliever.

ERIN: Where was this God the night I was raped. I screamed to Him for help.

JERICO: He heard you. You escaped. You're here.

ERIN: Don't force anything else on me. I'm so tired—

JERICO: I know.

ERIN: You could talk me me into believing anything— right now.

ACT TWO

JERICO: It's not you—it's this building that needs prayer. An exorcism of the whole place.

ERIN: Do it then. But I don't want to know—or be anywhere near when it's going on.

JERICO: You don't have to be.

ERIN: *(Sits on couch)* I'm so desperate, so helpless, so alone—I'm sitting here willing to listen to someone like you—

JERICO: Don't listen to me, then, listen only to your heart.

ERIN: My heart?

JERICO: Heart beats are the most soothing sound there is. Your very beginning—

ERIN: And your very end.

JERICO: Shhh.

ERIN: I don't even hear my heart anymore. Only when it cries out.

JERICO: I hear it crying out now—for love.

ERIN: You don't know what it's crying out for.

JERICO: Must be my own heart then. Listen—can't you hear it?

(JERICO *presses* ERIN's *hand against his heart.*)

ERIN: Nothing.

JERICO: Then it has to be put into words. My heart is trying to tell you—for so long, that, I love you.

ERIN: No—

JERICO: Shhh… Just listen… *(In rhythmic heartbeats)* I love you—I love you—I love you—

ERIN: Don't. *(Turns away)*

JERICO: Love can mend so many things… And when there are two in love—the greatest force in all the world.

ERIN: I've forgotten everything about love. Except my love for Heather.

JERICO: Can't you feel it?

ERIN: Something—

JERICO: Relax. Let it flow between us.

ERIN: I'm not ready.

JERICO: Try.

ERIN: I'm still afraid.

JERICO: I understand.

ERIN: I don't. I don't understand anything right now. Or what's taking place inside me.

JERICO: *(He holds her. Begins singing gently.)*
Come with Thy grace and heavenly aid
To fill the hearts which Thou has made,
To fill the hearts which Thou has made.

ERIN: I've never felt such a beautiful warm feeling flowing all through me.

JERICO: Nor I.

(ERIN and JERICO embrace.)

ERIN: In your arms—I feel so very safe.

JERICO: And loved. And protected.

ERIN: Oh God—I never thought I could feel this way again…

(End Scene Two)

ACT TWO 57

Scene Three

(One month later. Late afternoon. Building materials, paint cloths are cluttered near hall doorway. Gothic window has been repaired. Table is set with white tablecloth, candelabra.)

ERIN: *(Standing in open doorway)* What took you so long?

JERICO: I left as soon as you called. Where is the letter?

ERIN: I burned it.

JERICO: Why?

ERIN: I didn't want it around. Just touching it made me—

JERICO: All right. Repeat to me slowly, what the letter said.

ERIN: *(Deep breath)* "I am coming to get Heather. There is no way you can stop me…" He—he said she belonged to him—he wanted her—dreamed of her… There was no signature.

JERICO: *(Pause)* I need to ask this. You're sure all this happened. You actually received a letter. He wasn't playing his mind games again?

ERIN: Oh god, if you don't believe me…I flushed the ashes down the toilet. But I know I received that letter.

JERICO: I believe you.

ERIN: His letter was inside another envelope with different handwriting.

JERICO: Somebody must have smuggled it out for him.

ERIN: How did he know where we live?

JERICO: They have ways. Outside contacts.

ERIN: Who?

JERICO: Anybody. Women write to them, fall in love. Will do anything they ask.

ERIN: Why now? Everything was going so well since you moved into the house. Did your—whatever kind of rituals.

JERICO: Those rituals are what's kept him away these past weeks.

ERIN: Heather's nightmares stopped too. Now this.

JERICO: When's Heather coming home?

ERIN: Tomorrow. Sandra said she could stay one week.

JERICO: Doesn't give us much time.

ERIN: Do you think he's serious—about Heather?

JERICO: He very well could be. He's had years to think about it.

ERIN: What'll we do?

JERICO: I don't know yet… Too bad Heather couldn't stay at Sandra's a few more days.

ERIN: She was only staying there till her room got done. Sandra's got kids enough of her own.

JERICO: You have relatives—anywhere?

ERIN: None living.

JERICO: If I knew what he was planning.

ERIN: What about moving away somewhere—just temporary.

JERICO: He'd track you down. Somehow. Some time.

ERIN: Police—prison authorities, can't they do something?

JERICO: About what? You destroyed the letter.

ERIN: I feel—the way I did—right before the breakdown. Sweaty. Waves crashing around inside. Like I'm going to split apart.

JERICO: *(Holds her)* Relax. I'm here with you this time.

ACT TWO

ERIN: I know… This whole wonderful wonderful week—wiped out. I had such a grand dinner planned.

JERICO: Nothing's ever wasted. Look, once this house is finished—and I get that new job—we're going to get married—

ERIN: *(Breaking away)* I'm worried about what's happening now—not some fairytale future. *(Picks up dish, smashes it)* Broken! Smashed! He's destroyed everything worthwhile in my whole life. *(Begins sobbing)*

JERICO: I won't let him do that to you anymore.

ERIN: He'll destroy you too. And Heather.

JERICO: Then we have to outplan him.

ERIN: How?

JERICO: I'm not sure. *(Pause)* Think. Think. Think. Only my mind doesn't think like his. He has to be planning to escape.

ERIN: That's obvious.

JERICO: I'm sure he'll get in touch with you again before he would come here. He needs that perverted satisfaction, detailing his plan to his victims. He wants them so terrified they'll give in to anything.

ERIN: And what do I do then?

JERICO: If you hear from him? Call the police. Immediately!

ERIN: There's only two patrol cars in this whole town.

JERICO: Sheriff—F B I—It's a federal prison. Keep their number glued to the phone.

ERIN: And if he shows up?

JERICO: We'll have to set up some kind of plan. We don't let Heather alone—ever. One of us takes her to school, brings her home.

ERIN: Do you have a gun?

JERICO: No, I have a record. They don't allow it. Never owned one anyway.

ERIN: There has to be some way to protect ourselves.

JERICO: Wait—there's something I was going to tell you—later—the right time.

ERIN: What is it?

JERICO: Well, under this church is another room—

ERIN: I don't want to know—not now—

JERICO: Just listen… When I exorcised this church I wanted to make sure every inch was prayed over. I found this room—under the middle. It wasn't there before. The group that took over—must have dug it out. Held their rituals—or whatever there.

ERIN: We should never have moved here.

JERICO: It's all okay down there now. I cleaned it out. Put in flashlights, food, blankets—in case of a tornado. But you may have to use it.

ERIN: Hide—run—that's all I've done all my life.

JERICO: This will be the last time, I promise.

(Phone rings.)

ERIN: Probably Heather. *(Answers phone)* Hello… *(Listens. Hangs up. Slowly. Calmly.)* It was him. He's out of prison. He wanted me to know. *(Cracking)* How can he do this! After all these years— Why is he coming back into my life!!

JERICO: *(Goes to her. Tries to calm her.)* Just take it easy. You need to keep all your wits. Could you tell where he was calling from?

ERIN: No! He didn't tell me. He's an animal—on the loose again. I thought he was locked up for good!

ACT TWO   61

JERICO: Did it sound near or far?

ERIN: How should I know! The phone hasn't been working right since it was installed.

JERICO: Wherever he is—he's on his way here. Just a matter of when.

ERIN: He can't! He can't come here!

JERICO: I'm calling the police. *(Tries phone. Jiggles receiver.)* Damn! Line's dead—

ERIN: It doesn't work right, I told you—or, he's cut the line!

JERICO: He couldn't do it all that fast. I'll go call from the phone booth down the road.

ERIN: No! Don't leave me! I don't want to be alone.

JERICO: Tomorrow morning I'm moving you and Heather out of here. There's a cabin, up north, a friend would let me use it.

ERIN: What's the use. He'd only find us.

JERICO: We'll have to hope the police find him first. They'll be hot tracking him down. He doesn't care so much about getting caught as carrying out his plans.

ERIN: Maybe he was having someone else call—just to scare me.

JERICO: Maybe. But we don't know for sure.

ERIN: We don't know anything for sure.

(ERIN and JERICO both tense.)

JERICO: Shhh. Someone's out there.

ERIN: It's him!

JERICO: Quiet.

ERIN: He's here—outside!

(Pounding on door)

JERICO: I'll show you that trapdoor—it's under the hall rug—

(Voices heard)

HEATHER: Mom, it's me.

ERIN: *(Relieved)* It's only Heather and Sandra. What are they doing here?

(Knocking continues.)

HEATHER: Let me in.

ERIN: *(Unlocks door. Opens)* What—I thought you were staying with Jennifer till tomorrow. *(Hugs* HEATHER*)*

SANDRA: Was her idea. I was on my way to JoJo's, and Heather asks could she ride along. Got homesick. Said she wanted to go home today instead of tomorrow. So—

HEATHER: I wanted to surprise you.

ERIN: You certainly did that.

HEATHER: Hi Jerico. *(Hugs* JERICO*)* Boy do they have stuff you could fix at their place.

SANDRA: Say that again. But, looks like Jerico's been busy enough here. *(Noticing table)* You two weren't planning anything special tonight, were you?

ERIN: Nothing Heather would interrupt. I missed you so, honey. *(Hugs* HEATHER *again)*

HEATHER: I wanta see my new room. Right now—okay? It's all finished, isn't it?

JERICO: As of noon today.

ERIN: Beautifully finished. Waiting for a special little girl just like you.

HEATHER: I couldn't wait. I'm so excited— *(Drops Polly Wolly and duffel bag and exits to storage area)*

ACT TWO

SANDRA: So, two of you decided three can live cheaper than two.

ERIN: Something like that.

JERICO: Thanks, Sandra, for giving us this week together.

SANDRA: Didn't do it for you, Redbird.

ERIN: Well I thank you, more than I can ever tell.

SANDRA: Something the matter? You look kinda—frazzled. He didn't let you get much rest, did he.

ERIN: Well—a lot's been going on here.

SANDRA: I bet... Heather slept like a log. She and Jennifer giggled, sang—fought. Got along, just like sisters.

HEATHER: *(Running out)* I love it! I love it! And I don't ever have to sleep upstairs again?

ERIN: Not unless you want to. Jerico likes your old room.

HEATHER: He can have it. Just last week my new room was only a junky storeroom. Now—Jerico sure can work magic.

ERIN: *(Distraught)* Well—

SANDRA: Look, I gotta run. JoJo's waiting for me. Call you tomorrow.

ERIN: Tomorrow? Oh, sure.

HEATHER: Excuse me. I have to show Polly Wolly his new room. Thanks again, Mrs Porter. Maybe Jennifer can come and stay with me sometime—in my new posh place. *(Exits)*

SANDRA: Sure. I guess so.

ERIN: Sandra, could you, maybe— *(Stops)* Never mind. I hope she wasn't too much trouble.

SANDRA: Nah. I still like kids. And Sampson, he was decent enough. But, since I been taking karate—hey, when you gonna join me?

ERIN: I don't know.

JERICO: She has me to defend her now.

SANDRA: Huh! I'd still take karate.

ERIN: I'll call you.

JERICO: Blessings, Sandra. *(Goes into blessing motions)*

SANDRA: A right chop. *(Goes into karate chop)* Much better protection. *(Exits)*

ERIN: Bye. Thanks again. *(Closes door. Locks.)* Did I do okay? I was so nervous.

JERICO: You did just fine.

ERIN: I didn't expect Heather—

JERICO: *(Holds her)* Just calm down. Your heart is fluttering like a fearful bird.

HEATHER: *(Runs out of room, frightened)* Mom! Mom—I opened the shutters, and he was there! Looking in the window. His face, shining right through!

ERIN: What are you talking about?

JERICO: Come on. We'll check this out right now. We don't want anything frightening you in your new room. *(Exits)*

ERIN: Nothing happened here all week.

(ERIN *stands with* HEATHER *in kitchen doorway.*)

HEATHER: I know I saw it.

JERICO: *(Returns.)* Nothing. Come here. Let me show you.

HEATHER: I don't want to.

ACT TWO 65

JERICO: *(Takes her arm. They stand in doorway.)* See, when you stand here, the mirror reflects the window—the window reflects the mirror. What you saw was probably only one of your animals—distorted—and it surprised you.

HEATHER: *(Hesitant)* I still thought I saw his face.

JERICO: I made special inside shutters that lock real tight. I'm locking them right now. *(Exits to room)*

HEATHER: *(Entering with* ERIN*)* I wasn't afraid all week.

ERIN: *(Begins unzipping* HEATHER's *duffel bag)* We have a special surprise for you. Jerico's friend has a cabin—in the woods—and we're going there tomorrow morning—for a vacation.

HEATHER: I don't want to go. I have my own room now. I want to stay here.

ERIN: Well, I thought—all your clothes are already packed. *(Zips zipper back and forth nervously)*

JERICO: *(Returning)* Everything tight and secure.

HEATHER: It better be.

JERICO: Just one more thing, Heather. We found a tornado shelter under this church. Cleaned it out, fixed it up. So, anytime there's tornado warnings—you go down there and you'll be safe and sound.

HEATHER: I don't want to go down into any tornado shelter or any cabin in the woods either.

JERICO: Hey, I promised I'd show you Indian ways. We can build a teepee, campfire.

HEATHER: Well, maybe. It's just that I missed my house here. I didn't think I would. But I did. And you too, Jerico. I have a whole family now, like everybody else.

ERIN: Families go camping—stay at cabins.

HEATHER: Okay. But only for a day or so.

JERICO: You may like it so well—

HEATHER: I probably won't.

ERIN: We have to let Jerico help make decisions now too.

HEATHER: *(Petulant)* Okay.

ERIN: So glad to have you back.

(ERIN *hugs* HEATHER.)

HEATHER: *(Breaks away)* So much stuff to tell you. First, I decided I don't need animals under my bed anymore. Jennifer doesn't sleep with any animals.

ERIN: That's wonderful.

(Phone rings. ERIN *jumps.)*

JERICO: I'll get it. Hello… *(Authoritative voice)* No, this is the Church of the Holy Ghost—

HEATHER: Is he being funny?

ERIN: Shhh.

JERICO: Yes… Yes… Thank you for the warning. We'll be sure to make preparations.

(JERICO *hangs up. Scene speeds up.)*

ERIN: Who was it?

JERICO: Civil Warning Patrol. Tornado watch. Hurry! You and Heather get down into that tornado shelter. Right now!

HEATHER: I didn't hear any sirens.

ERIN: Is it close?

(JERICO *nods.)*

ERIN: How close?

JERICO: Very close. There's not much time. Go!

ERIN: Come on, Heather.

ACT TWO

HEATHER: Geez, I come home—to try out my new room, and right away hafta go down into some dumb old basement.

ERIN: Get going!

HEATHER: It better not be for long.

ERIN: Coming Jerico?

JERICO: You two go ahead. I have to secure the building.

ERIN: You have to come with us.

JERICO: Will you just go!

ERIN: You can't fight a tornado alone. Even you know that.

JERICO: I won't be alone. *(Clasps hands in prayer)* Now get out of here! I need to prepare.

HEATHER: Come on, Mom. He's really mad.

ERIN: *(Torn between the two)* If you don't come down— I'm coming back after you.

JERICO: Just go!

(They exit.)

(JERICO *begins reciting the "Our Father" in a clear strong voice as he hastily makes preparations. Lights four large candles atop bookshelves.)*

(He hastily nails two large pieces of construction wood into a crude cross. Stands it in front of sofa. Takes Bible out from under sofa. Holds it up as he continues.)

JERICO: Our Father, Who art in Heaven,
Hallowed be thy name.
Thy kingdom come, Thy will be done,
On earth as it is in Heaven.
Give us this day our daily bread,
And forgive us our trespasses
As we forgive those who trespass against us,

And lead us not into temptation
But deliver us from evil...

(As he says "evil", there's a loud crackle and blue flash. The lights go dim, as if a power line were cut. Window and candles emit the only light.)

JERICO: *(Shouts, holding up Bible as he finishes)* For thine is the kingdom, and the power, and the glory, Forever and ever. Amen!

(He falls to his knees in prayer.)

(End Scene Three)

Scene Four

(A few minutes later. JERICO, *still in prostrate position, praying. There's loud knocking on door.* JERICO *tenses, waits. Knocking is now fierce pounding.)*

JERICO: Who's there?

MAN: Just open the damn door, or I'll blow it off its hinges.

JERICO: *(Rises. Staring straight forward. Bible raised above his head. Slowly and positively.)* This is a church of God.

MAN: I know they're still in there. I been watching the road, all evening.

JERICO: *(Louder)* This is a church of God!

MAN: You open this door. `Cause if you don't, I have fire bombs, grenades. I can set this whole place ablaze in two minutes. I love to see people run out of burning buildings. Haven't done that in a long time.

JERICO: *(Opens door slowly. Chain is still on.)* This is a church of God. Nothing evil is allowed to enter here. *(Gives blessing sign)*

ACT TWO

(With a fierce cry and brute strength the MAN *forces the door wide open. He stands there, gun in hand. He's wearing a dark gray hooded sweatshirt and sweatpants. The hood covers most of his face.)*

(He quickly closes the door and locks it. Stepping into room:)

MAN: Where are they?

JERICO: Who?

MAN: The woman? The kid?

JERICO: I told you this is a church of God, a sanctuary from all evil.

MAN: *(Goes into rampant rage. Blood-curdling scream. Picks up cross, spits on it. Tears it apart with his bare hands, and viciously throws the parts to the floor behind.)* This is what I think of your God! *(Grabs* JERICO *by the throat)* You tell me where they are. Because I'll kill you if you don't—and I'll find them anyway. Because none of your gods are stronger than the bullets in this gun.

JERICO: I am here alone.

MAN: *(Goes into new rage. Grabs Bible, throws it down, stomps on it.)* Your Bible—I crush it under my feet! *(Another cry)*

JERICO: And still it will live.

MAN: I can blow you away like nothing. But I want them both—alive.

JERICO: They're not here.

MAN: The child's mine. I'm taking her with me—after I kill the mother—the bitch.

JERICO: They have the Lord's shield of protection surrounding them.

MAN: There is no protection. Not from me. I been planning this day, ever since I was locked up. I have it all worked out, and nothing's going to stop me.

JERICO: Your power stopped, once you stepped inside this church.

MAN: Let me just test my powers then. *(Goes into whirling dervish dance with shouts and cries. All of a sudden the lights begin flashing on and off, then stay on.)* They're in this building... The depths of hell are under this building and I will descend and find them. I shall go into hell for my victims this time. *(Laughs viciously. Hands over eyes as if in trance.)* I see a rug. Under the rug is a trapdoor. The handle, so cleverly concealed. It's— that way. In that hall. *(Pause)* Now do you believe in my special powers—preacher?

JERICO: I kneel to someone infinitely more powerful. *(Starts to kneel)*

MAN: You stupid— *(Kicks JERICO in the knees. He falls forward.)* Now—get up, and move ahead of me.

JERICO: *(Back to kneeling.)* I have not yet finished my prayers.

MAN: Get up! And cut the crap.

JERICO: *(Looking up)* Amen.

MAN: I said "Get up!" *(Jerks JERICO's head back, then grabs his hands and pulls him up roughly. Grabbing his face.)* I'll tear your face from you, you let out any more sounds.

JERICO: Lord the Almighty, help us!

MAN: You son of a bitch—I'll get rid of you once and for all. *(Slowly releases JERICO, still holding his arm)* No. I want you around to watch. Yeah. Tape your eyes wide open. And make you watch everything. First, the woman. I can do wicked things to women. But, I've had her before. It's the child I want this time. I've never had a child before. And this one belongs to me! *(Wild laugh)*

ACT TWO

JERICO: Would you bargain my life for theirs?

MAN: Bargain? *(Throws* JERICO *down)* I can wipe you out with a flick of my tongue or a bullet from this gun. But I still want you to watch. I like it better when I have an audience.

JERICO: *(Kneels)* Our Father—

MAN: *(Pulls* JERICO *up roughly)* I told you to get moving. I don't have all night. I'm getting heated up just thinking about everything.

JERICO: *(Looks up and away)* Dear God—

MAN: Don't even try for help of that kind—or using that phone. I cut the phone wires, power lines too. But, just to make sure. *(Rips phone wires from wall)* Now, let's get to those women.

JERICO: How can there be so much evil in one man?

MAN: Because I made a pact with the devil, a long time ago. All my power comes from him. He's the one who brought me here, now, and all the nights before. Now get moving! My heat's getting higher each second.

(JERICO *slowly starts to move, then turns quicky and lunges for the gun. There's a short struggle. A shot is fired and* JERICO *staggers and falls to floor.)*

MAN: *(Crouching, gun still aimed)* You bastard!

(Immediately following the shot, ERIN *appears in doorway. She quickly picks up one board of broken cross and strikes* MAN *across the back of his head. He keels over with a cry of rage and pain, gun falling from his hand.)*

*(*ERIN *continues striking him on his head over and over, screaming out all the agonies pent up since the night of the rape. They explode in a violent physical and verbal frenzy.)*

ERIN: I'll kill you! I'll kill you once and for all! So you won't ever be able to hurt anyone again.

JERICO: *(Crawls over weakly)* Erin—

ERIN: *(With each blow.)* —This is for all those women chained in that room! —For what you've done to me that night and every night after! —For torturing my child! —Men like you don't deserve to live! The worst slime—The lowest beasts that ever existed! —You should be castrated the minute you were born! *(Exhausted, collapses in sobbing heap)*

JERICO: *(Takes wood from her)* Erin—no more.

ERIN: *(Great panic)* Blood—his blood's all over— *(Screaming)* I don't want it touching me.

JERICO: Cover him.

(JERICO *points.* ERIN *covers* MAN *with black paint drop cloth. Weakening voice.)*

JERICO: Get Heather—tell her to go to Sandra's—

ERIN: *(Goes to* JERICO*)* Oh my god! You need an ambulance.

JERICO: Hurry—

(ERIN *exits quickly.)*

(*There's movement under the cloth.* JERICO *strains to reach gun on the floor. The* MAN *partially rises with cloth over him.* JERICO *shoots once and collapses. There is one last cry as* MAN *crumples under cloth.)*

ERIN: *(Guiding* HEATHER *quickly)* Don't look! Don't stop! Just run down the road, fast as you can. Hurry!!

(*Once* HEATHER*'s out,* ERIN *rushes to* JERICO*)*

ERIN: I heard shots—I thought—

JERICO: He was still moving. He's gone now.

ERIN: What about you—

JERICO: I don't know…

ERIN: *(Holding his head)* If I lose you—oh god—

ACT TWO

JERICO: *(Slowly)* Why didn't you go down into the cellar, like I asked?

ERIN: I couldn't leave you here alone—to face him. I couldn't take the chance of losing you—

JERICO: I feel— *(Stops)*

ERIN: *(Crying softly)* Don't die, Jerico. Not now.

JERICO: Pray for me, Erin. I'm too weak to do it myself.

ERIN: I don't know how. I've forgotten how to pray.

JERICO: Just ask God— *(Voice dies)*

ERIN: Oh God—I don't know prayer words anymore—I don't know how to ask you—but please, don't let Jerico die. You don't need him up there. But Heather and I—we need him down here. So very much.

JERICO: Press your hand—here—against the bleeding. I can't anymore.

ERIN: *(Sobbing)* Save him! Oh God, please save him!

HEATHER: *(Bursts into room)* They're coming, Mom. They're coming. *(Looks at scene)* What happened?

ERIN: Come here, Heather. Come here, and pray with me.

HEATHER: Pray?

ERIN: For Jerico. For us.

(HEATHER *goes to* ERIN. *They are huddled together in one close group.*)

ERIN: *(Still pressing* JERICO's *wound)* Lord help us—Father in heaven—help us. *(Repeats over and over in a litany of anguished pleas)* Lord help us—Lord help us—Lord help us—

HEATHER: *(Holds* JERICO's *hand. Breaks into soft singing.)*
Oh, I went down South for to see my gal—
Singing Polly Wolly Doodle all the day—

Oh my Polly am a purty gal—
Singing Polly Wolly Doodle all the day.
Fare thee well, fare thee well—
(Repeats softly over and over) Fare thee well

(In the distance sirens are heard. ERIN's *praying,* HEATHER's *singing, are echoed and reechoed, coming from all sides of the room.)*

(Faintly in the background, organ music begins playing. Prayers and singing blend together as a church choir singing.)

(Sirens get closer. Suddenly bright flashing and circling lights stream in through the gothic window. They circle brighter and wider, then stop as the whole room is bathed in golden light. All sound subsides.)

(Faintly and almost ethereally the organ music and choir singing, heard at the beginning, rise softly in the distance.)

CHOIR: Oh come, come, come, come…

(Slow fade to black)

(Curtain)

END OF PLAY

www.ingramcontent.com/pod-product-compliance
Lightning Source LLC
Chambersburg PA
CBHW071742040426
42446CB00012B/2438